D0209372

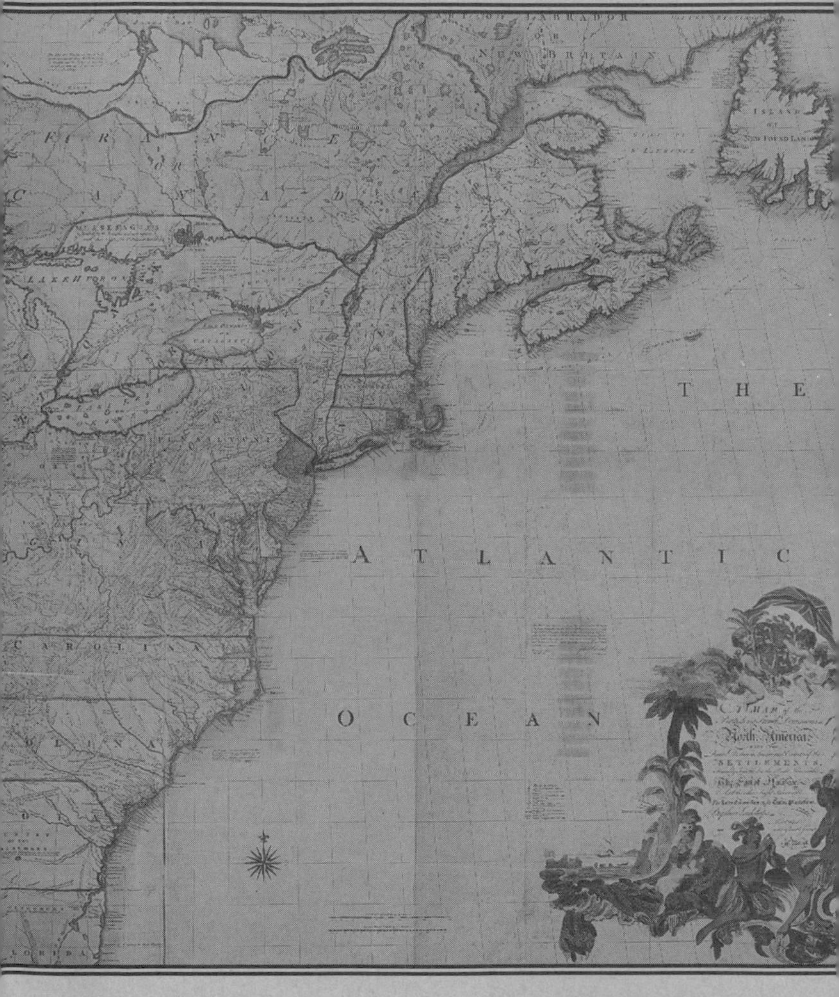

THE
ATLANTIC
OCEAN
ISLAND OF NEW FOUND LAND
CAROLINA
North America
SETTLEMENTS

America's Founding Secret

Andrew –

I heard the author speak on this subject last summer and was fascinated. I hope you are.

Jim

Christmas, '03

Scottish penny commemorating Adam Smith,
1723–1790, by P. Kempson

Scottish penny commemorating Adam Smith,
1723–1790, by P. Kempson

America's Founding Secret

What the
SCOTTISH
ENLIGHTENMENT
Taught Our
FOUNDING
FATHERS

ROBERT W. GALVIN

ROWMAN & LITTLEFIELD PUBLISHERS, INC.
Lanham • Boulder • New York • Oxford

ROWMAN & LITTLEFIELD PUBLISHERS, INC.

Published in the United States of America
by Rowman & Littlefield Publishers, Inc.
A Member of the Rowman & Littlefield Publishing Group
4720 Boston Way, Lanham, Maryland 20706
www.rowmanlittlefield.com

12 Hid's Copse Road
Cumnor Hill, Oxford OX2 9JJ, England

Copyright © 2002 by Robert W. Galvin

All rights reserved. No part of this publication may be reproduced,
stored in a retrieval system, or transmitted in any form or by any means,
electronic, mechanical, photocopying, recording, or otherwise, without
the prior permission of the publisher.

British Library Cataloguing in Publication Information Available

Library of Congress Cataloging-in-Publication Data

Galvin, Robert W.
  America's founding secret : what the Scottish enlightenment taught our
founding fathers / Robert W. Galvin
    p. cm.
Includes bibliographical references and index.
  ISBN 0-7425-2280-6 (alk. paper)
  1. United States—Intellectual life—18 th century. 2. Political
science—United States—History—18th century. 3.
Enlightenment—Scotland. 4. Scotland—Intellectual life—18th century.
5. Enlightenment—United States. 6. United
States—Civilization—Scottish influences. I. Title.
  E163 .G35 2002
  973—dc21

                                                        2002003367

Printed in the United States of America

∞™ The paper used in this publication meets the minimum requirements
of American National Standard for Information Sciences—Permanence of
Paper for Printed Library Materials, ANSI/NISO Z39.48-1992.

This Book Is Dedicated to
Great Personal Teachers

Contents

Illustrations

Acknowledgments

Professors Robert Goldwin and the late Martin Diamond's role in seeding my interest in the constitutionalizing of our country is detailed in the opening commentary of "Why These Essays?"

Others like them inspired me individually, led by Professor George Doriot, the dean of the Boston area's distinguished business school leaders a score of years ago, with his leveraging concepts like "Spread Hope"—a sine qua non for founders and other leaders.

Two texts, the autobiography of Bernard Baruch and *Your Creative Power* by Alex Osborn, the cofounder of the preeminent advertising agency Batten, Barton, Durstine, and Osborn, were incomparable guides to my thinking process. Baruch, a successful early-1900s financier and advisor to many presidents, practiced and advocated counterintuitive thinking (challenging the evident), and Osborn wrote the most useful methodology on how to be purposefully and frequently creative.

My father was the model inspiration as founder of our company. He nourished my zeal for uncommon thinking with his profound common sense learned from early failures and the tenacity to overcome.

America's Founding Secret

Why These Essays?
Who Made the Difference?
Where Could Their Thoughts Lead?

The two hundredth anniversary of the Declaration of Independence raised the question "How does one celebrate? March in a parade? Hold a banquet? Publish ads?" These responses seemed insufficient.

Long before 1976, I was fascinated by the founding process, particularly the founding of our corporation by my father. It dawned on me that a "celebrative" formal study of the founding of our nation would be rewarding for a multi-age gathering of our family. After all, the Declaration of Independence was a literal preamble to the constitutional launching of our country.

These thoughts set me to outlining an agenda for six monthly home dinner meetings. The topics selected were the Declaration itself, the Articles of Confederation, the Constitution, the Federalist Papers, the anti-Federalist Papers, and slavery.

Professors were engaged as proctors. Reading was prepared for each of the sixteen members of the family. Discussants respected the "one voice at a time" format during the four-hour gatherings that yielded in-depth, inspiring inputs and insights by all participants.

Earlier public policy lessons imparted to me were equivalent stimulators. These focused on the Constitution and the Federalist Papers and the scholarship of Dr. Robert Goldwin, then a member of the faculty of the University of Chicago, and Dr. Martin Diamond (deceased), then of the Claremont College group, who was preeminently knowledgeable about the Federalist Papers.

Bob Goldwin, a friend over the years and a recent resident scholar of the American Enterprise Institute, Washington, D.C., shared with me inspiring conversations in the 1960s, as well as his many texts over later years, detailing the thinking and the interplay of our extraordinary constitutional authors. About the same era, Martin Diamond was guest of honor at adult dinner parties in our home where we encouraged evening-long, lively debates of self-appointed Federalists and anti-Federalists.

Much of those scholars' influence is reflected in paragraphs on pages 38 and 39 in this book. With the passing of decades, I cannot separate what expressions in those paragraphs may have been fashioned at my rhetorical initiation, versus others that should be expressly attributable to Robert Goldwin and/or Martin Diamond. If, as is likely, I have retained and expressed here any of their thoughtful phrasing of the content that they taught me, it is simply subliminal manifestation of my appreciation for and acknowledgment of their lasting influence.

The other themes and factors in these essays are an aggregation of selected personal studies over the years and periodic thought processing. The role of the Scottish Enlightenment was identified and studied later. The combination of all of the above suggested to me that the unique story of the confluence of multiple interactors influencing the minds and energies of the founders themselves deserves the accent of these essays. It details how it came to pass that for the first time in history, a government was conceived and defined with a purposeful intent as to its affordability by promoting economic progress in commerce based on private capital means and thus the likely sustaining of a large republic and the freedom it espoused.

The lessons of the Scots and the lessons of the founders are as useable today as yesterday.

Could they be the seeds of enlightened refounding of certain upgradeable countries that early on inevitably must renew?

about to read. I'd given thousands of other speeches. These four roused the listeners. In each case, at least a majority of the attendees went out of their way, sought me out to exclaim, "This is so new to me! How enlightening! Thank you!"

Thus the title "The *Untold* Story of the Founding of the U.S. Republic." Untold to the citizens, thoughtful citizens.

Ironically, there is a breadth and depth of scholarship existent and in process including on the Scottish Enlightenment featured here on the early pages. But mostly this occurs among the scholars. Every historian who read early versions of this manuscript objected to my use of the adjective "untold." They pleaded that they are aware of and are publishing related material, so I credit them but point out graciously that "they are only talking to themselves."

I have no credentials as a scholar, although I have some as a citizen. As a citizen, I wish to fill a significant void in our citizen understanding of our history.

The factors and principles that these essays emphasize have been innocently obscured. Yet, they have been transcending in their consequence throughout the first two centuries of our statehood. They are likely to be more influential in the next century by their prospective effect at home and elsewhere. If they have been so effective in obscurity, how much greater benefit can their more prominent, conscious endorsement stimulate?

The story starts with and radiates from the Scottish Enlightenment:

- The grandest aggregation of leading scholars from virtually all then existing fields of knowledge
- Thinking together in one locale
- During a compressed era of time

The profound interdisciplinary wisdom that cascaded from its midst incomparably

James Watt

Adam Smith

Francis Hutcheson

David Hume

Several others were mixed in with prominent theologians and political leaders. In fact, many of the named also had strong religious preferences and advocacies, while others pronounced unapologetically contrarian heresies. Above all, all of them were teachers and/or teachers of teachers, including each other.

In addition to classroom lectures, scholastic society meetings, and publications, these scholars regularly honed their thinking at evening discussion clubs whose interests ranged from a specialty subject with purposeful focus to the broadest of general issues. Small in size, those meetings typically engaged a handful to a score of thinkers/debaters sipping ale and puffing pipes.

The stimulation was boundless. It echoed throughout the entire intellectual community. Its concepts were refined with each passing year, resonating across the seas.

The Enlightenment can be said to have begun in Glasgow with the publication in

1725 of Francis Hutcheson's "Inquiry into the Originals of the Ideas of Beauty and Virtue." That essay's insights about nature and humanity, a virtual preamble to the wealth of thinking to follow, were beyond classic.

"Beginnings" have their seedings.[1] Hutcheson and the others among the early wave of the Enlightened consistently demonstrated their keen disposition as learners from the likes of the John Lockes and the Isaac Newtons who had preceded them.

In addition, they were conditioned by a Scottish society in ferment, *as usual*, following centuries of struggles for ascendancy by many would-be royal families (Stuarts, Tudors, others); frequent wars with England winning/losing independence; on-again, off-again alliances with

---

1. Reference to the following essay "How Did the Scottish Enlightenment Come to Be?" is relevant.

France with an attendant unwelcomed Roman Catholic influence; and deep-seated religious resentments within many of the strengthening Protestant sects, each seemingly outdoing the other by invoking "their fear of God" discipline into each church's followers.

These fermentings eventually were tempered somewhat. A moderate strain of sobriety between England and Scotland began to infuse key leaders. The Parliaments of both countries passed laws uniting the two kingdoms in 1707. However, the united kingdoms were obliged to yet survive two final, bitter, but unsuccessful rebellions in 1715 and 1745.

The coexisting intellectual ferment stirred a vigorous life of its own that attracted the leading scholars of Europe into its cerebral and geographic web. It fueled their more ardent search for betterments in their long-suffering society.

This search included a scan of the predicaments of other somewhat similar "states." After more than a century of benign neglect, the American colonies began to suffer the oppression of the English imperial yoke in a fashion somewhat similar to that of Scotland. Frequent comparisons were analyzed in hopes of finding common cause and cure.

A most uncommon cause surfaced. It offered possible consequences in the all-consuming contests among religious sects at home. Various sects began to imagine the possibility of greater evangelical success in the "overseas province" than a competing creed, which success they surmised could reflect in a stronger following of their particular flock back in Scotland. Favorable reaction by colonists became a principal hope of those who would reform religion at home.

This prompted increased assignments of clerics to colonial projects and residencies. The underlying motive differed from the well-known quests for religious freedoms that drove so many others to America's shores. Thus, this development turned into a mid-1700s campaign to capture a greater share of the minds and souls of men. Who better than the parsons, ministers, and such to lead this charge and also to double in the welcome role of general teacher?

Year after year, as more of these church-oriented assignments were assumed, these theologians/teachers or teachers/theologians who themselves had been the students or audience of the Enlightened became prominent conveyors of the thinking fed by this uncommon enlightened source of all-encompassing ideas and wisdom.

The networking conditions among the learned and learning Scots were ideal. Virtually all the influential thinkers were in frequent contact with each other in just two main communities. These communities, Edinburgh and Glasgow, had populations of less than thirty thousand each. Thus, almost everyone could know almost every other body and the enlightening thoughts that flowed freely among them.

And so it followed that an "intellectual gospel" spread to the colonies.

By the time each of them was sixteen years of age, Thomas Jefferson, James Madison, and Alexander Hamilton were being schooled by Scots simply because it was a meritorious, available, natural option. Donald Robertson, a Scot who had studied at Aberdeen and Edinburgh Universities, was one to whom Madison voiced high praise for the schooling Robertson had rendered to him. Francis Allison, a pupil of Hutcheson, came to the colonies in 1735 as a tutor to the Dickenson family of Maryland and later taught at least three signers of the Declaration of Independence. Many youths of the mid-1700s were similarly trained through secondary education.

One of the more prominent educators from Scotland, if not the most respected, was Rev. John Witherspoon, who became the president of the University of New Jersey at Princeton. One of Madison's professors, he was renowned for his toleration of the more contentious societal views of Hume and Robertson. A conservative by nature, he saw to the balanced exposure of his students to all pre-Enlightenment and Enlightenment thinking. In his autobiography, Edinburgh-educated Dr. Benjamin Rush wrote that Witherspoon "gave a new turn to education" in "taste and correctness. . . . It was easy to distinguish his pupils everywhere whenever they spoke or wrote for the public."

Scottish moral philosophy was an integral part of the curricula of most American colleges of the time. William Small at the College of William and Mary, professor of moral philosophy and rhetoric, read with and taught Thomas Jefferson for his first two university years and carried on a close scholarly association following Jefferson's studies at Princeton, also shaped by Witherspoon. Jefferson later credited Small for much of the success he achieved.

Thomas Jefferson

James Madison

Alexander Hamilton

John Witherspoon

William Small

The effects of Scottish thinking were eminent in many ordinary ways and places. For example, when the Continental Congress wanted a list of books available for the use of the Congress, it appointed a committee chaired by James Madison and including John Lowell of Massachusetts and Madison's former mentor, John Witherspoon. The list, submitted in January 1783, included Scottish authors throughout—Hume, Smith, Ferguson, Miller, and others—most of whose books Madison, Witherspoon, and Jefferson also personally owned and studied.

A transcending historic impact was the surfacing of a principle that was to shape a critical fundamental of our emergent free society. It flowed from an integration of newly emphatic and integrated thinking that called for the increased role of commerce in planning for a nation's development and affordability.

At the beginning of this essay, reference was made to this being a rarely told, even an *un*told, story of our republic's founding. Of course, many of us know some important parts of that history, including the role of Adam Smith's prominent invisible-hand thesis inscribed in *The Wealth of Nations* and the Lockean principles that predated that publication.

What is inadequately appreciated is the common thread referenced by many of the leaders of the Enlightenment of the "link between intellectual and economic development." The links in their chain of thinking were frequent and meaty. Example: David Hume, among others, analyzed economic history to its essence. He and others identified and defined four stages in the development of mankind and social order. They were hunting-gathering, pasturage, farming, and commerce—a painstakingly long evolution from a lower to higher standard of living.

It is significant to note again how pervasive Enlightenment thinking and rhetoric became. While president of the

United States, James Madison addressed the Agricultural Society of Virginia and said in context of a broad-ranging speech, "The hunter becomes the herdsman, the latter a follower of the plow and the last repairing to manufactory or workshops." Others wrote similarly— even inspiringly. Witherspoon's theme was his "linking commerce to piety." Jay G. Prokop, a later scholar of the scholars, writes, "The great achievement of the Scottish school of sociological historians was the recognition that a commercial organization of society had rendered obsolete much that had been believed about society before."

The dynamic of this class of thinking is further illustrated by an effort at reciprocal influence back to Scotland. William Thom, a close associate of Witherspoon with strong commercial convictions, recommended that the University of Glasgow revise its curriculum, upgrading and featuring commercial training.

It is not as if the Scots were presuming to have discovered commerce as such. Rather, somewhat analogous to the puzzlement and promise over the new economy versus the old economy that demands our attention as we start the twenty-first century, their eighteenth-century systems thinking described a vision or a hope or a dream (really a proposition) that commerce, which had been around for centuries but influenced just a small proportion of a population's way of life, could expand—and for the better.

No longer was commerce to be looked upon with suspicion. Francis Hutcheson argued that the increased standards of living promoted by commerce would stimulate virtuous behavior.

All at one time and all in one place, the enlightened could envision (in fact, they could hardly help but stumble over their combinable phenomenal achievements) increased power from reliable engines, new materials from new chemistry, finer building construction, transportation infrastructure upgrades, better yields from the earth, health benefits, and more. The sciences were coming of a more useful age. Fresh social, economic, and political concepts offered the promise of operational systems that could harmonize all the above to satisfy beneficial and needed useful arts (business) intents.

Scottish scholars were keenly aware that each nation at times, and most nations and empires all of the time, had afforded themselves only by force, and more often than not, they were founded by force. The synonyms for *force* at the time were *plunder, piracy,* and *conquest*—not exactly an acceptable way of the world. To these scholars, nations had to find a way to be affordable civilly. Agrarian societies (herding, etc.) held little promise of fulfillment. So, there was a practical realization that commerce had to and could become an equal among equals in the makeup of subsystems of civil and sustaining nations. This concept was to have a dramatic impact on the constitutional intent of the soon-to-be United States of America.

In defending the new constitution then under consideration for adoption in October 1787, Alexander Hamilton wrote:

IT HAS BEEN FREQUENTLY REMARKED, THAT IT SEEMS TO HAVE BEEN RESERVED TO THE PEOPLE OF THIS COUNTRY, BY THEIR CONDUCT AND EXAMPLE, TO DECIDE THE IMPORTANT QUESTION, WHETHER SOCIETIES OF MEN ARE REALLY CAPABLE OR NOT, OF ESTABLISHING GOOD GOVERNMENT FROM REFLECTION AND CHOICE, OR WHETHER THEY ARE FOREVER DESTINED TO DEPEND, FOR THEIR POLITICAL CONSTITUTIONS, ON ACCIDENT AND FORCE.

Reference has been made to the oppressions that similarly throttled Scotland and the colonies. To both, resistance was an all-consuming subject. Francis Hutcheson, among others, had an overwhelming philosophical and stimulating influence by his endorsement of and arguments for "The Right to Resistance" (a major essay). His and the other advocates' words were casting a die.

By the mid-1770s, the rebels among the colonists hardly needed any more scholarly justification to resist their king. They declared their independence!

This courageous part of the founding story is well known. Yet, few of us are familiar with a curious detail—the proliferation of pre-1776 rhetoric, substantially from the pens of Scottish scholars (again, notably Hutcheson), that composed persuasive, documented justifications for oppressed people to assert their independence.

Thomas Jefferson unquestionably deserves high praise for the superbly reasoned, integrated, and phrased Declaration of Independence text. It should simply be noted that sprinkled throughout

Enlightenment essays are multiple paragraphs similar to each other and not so different from Jefferson's.

Jefferson readily acknowledged that his ideas were not original. He drew upon the Scottish and English writings of the earlier advocates not to find new principles or arguments but to place before mankind the common sense, tone, and spirit of the subject. It is interesting to note that Jefferson here refers to "the common sense of the subject." The overall Scottish Enlightenment ideas were known both then and now as the "common sense" school of philosophy. Furthermore, Thomas Paine, in drafting his monumental essay advocating independence, intended to title it "Plain Truth." When, however, Scottish-educated Benjamin Rush suggested "Common Sense" instead, Paine readily accepted the change.

So far our story has revolved primarily around the Scots because, as referenced earlier, their influence was incomparable.

But incomparable leaves open dissimilar influences from the colonists' many friends and opponents in England, challenging sociopolitical stirrings in France, and the then-current European philosophical thinking reflecting all the way back to the Greeks.

Those great minds among the founders and those who dared great deeds now faced the daunting task of writing the rules for their long-sought free society.

Society

Society is a grand and dynamic system of people and institutions. It is grand because of its size and complexity and dynamic because it is ever changing among many choices.

A system is typically made up of subsystems. The subsystems of society are elements such as education that trains, military that defends, religion that redeems, and others.

Two of the others at the heart of the "founder" story are business and government. Let us position them.

Business

I define *business* as that subsystem of society that honorably serves the needs of customers at a profit. When you decode this definition and relate business to the other equally important subsystems, you note that business is the only subpart or agent or institution that generates wealth.

Many subsystems bring unique values to the whole. That is their natural vital role. It does not make one better than others. Business benefits from the contributions of others. Its nature, when honorably and capably operated, is to produce an increase in tangible, transactionable wealth that becomes the principal "currency" to afford government and all the other subsystems that government regulates.

Government

Government applies civic order within the system of people and institutions, variously allowing or disallowing degrees of active pursuits. The early lessons of government came from the Greeks. To them, the chief goal of government was the excellence of people. When Plato spoke of human nature, he meant what human beings could become.

The Greeks' preamble to governance was the view that some authority had to know what goodness was and prescribe it as a duty; from the performance of that duty, a right was earned. Note that in that thesis of governance, a right had to be *earned*. Now there may be some limited appeal to that concept. However, for centuries it has yielded nothing but lordly tyranny. The lords, who thought themselves the better, sparingly granted rights and privileges to individuals in the multitude whom they deigned to be less worthy.

Shortly before the Scottish Enlightenment, a philosophy emerged from the Thomases, Lockes, Montesquieus, and others. (Please watch for the early thinking of George Buchanan cited in the next essay.) When John Locke spoke of people, he meant what human beings are to begin with: simple creatures of nature, bestowed with life, the right to be free to protect it, to sustain it by their voluntary labor, and to possess the fruits of that labor. Those efforts and fruits required civic order for which enlightened thinkers concluded that the chief goal of government should be to protect those rights that were inalienable. Note in this view, rights herein are a *given*!

Our founding fathers puzzled over the form of government best suited to that principle and the new country. There was a clear leaning to a republic. The problem was that the only models then available to evaluate were small republics. Our prospective country loomed large. Would a large republic sustain liberties and support itself?

James Madison took up the question on the eve of the Constitutional Convention about to convene in 1787. He was not alone, for this was a subject not overlooked by others. In his 1752 essay "Idea of a Perfect Commonwealth," David Hume outlined a theory that if a large republic could ever be formed, it was the more likely to sustain freedom.

Hume reasoned that people had natural self-interests. Those with similar self-interests would be attracted to each other. These associations he called *factions*. Multiple factions would emerge within a large population. Various factions would offset others. This recurring phenomenon would prevent the aggregation of an oppressive majority.

This and a prescriptive system of checks and balances would make for a long-living republic with the rights of all manner of minorities optimally and increasingly respected. Madison and his peers were so convinced.

They expressed related thoughts, forthrightly. "Men are not angels," they said. "Desire for personal, selfish advantage is not only something to be tolerated but is a force to be put to work for public good." This opinion was not an endorsement of illicit behavior but rather a pragmatic acknowledgment of tolerable conduct that they believed would be self-correcting. In fact, somewhat like Witherspoon, who saw shades of piety resident in commerce, some founders hoped that commerce based on freedom of choice would nurture virtue.

An unparalleled historic effect of this profound association of thoughts was that our founding fathers were the first founders of a country to grasp the importance of basing a society's governance on a foundation cornerstone of commerce, capital, and a growing economy. This compelling purpose—a special role for business—is too little appreciated.

The philosophers and the founders understood that the pursuit of plenty from self-interest developments is essential to affording a growing republic and its enduring qualities. One of the more evident expressions of intent and providers of thrust to this purpose is ordained in the constitutional provision called the Progress Clause or the Inventors Clause, in Article I, Section 8, of the Constitution. It reads, "The Congress shall have power to promote the progress of science and useful arts by securing for limited times to authors and inventors the exclusive *right* to their respective writings and discoveries."

Think of that intent!

VEST POWER TO A CONGRESS TO PROMOTE PROGRESS FROM SCIENCE AND THE USEFUL ARTS—BUSINESS.

The progress in sciences by the Enlightenment thinkers and others was well known. Its potential for gainful exploitations through the likes of "manufactory and the workshop" was promising. The latter terms obviously were metaphors for the emerging useful arts and new key processes of business.

Think further of this concept:

[GRANT] PROPERTY RIGHTS DERIVED FROM THE CREATIVE LABOR OF THE MIND.

One may not remember or may never have heard that this is the only right—yes, the *only* right—granted by the Constitution. In fact, it is the only place where the word *right* is written in the body of the Constitution.

"What about the Bill of Rights?" you say. Even those amendments grant no rights! The so-called Bill of Rights is composed as a prohibitive or cast in negative terminology. It starts with the words "Congress shall make no laws" (and here I paraphrase) restricting or abridging freedoms of speech, assembly, or religion that man inalienably always possessed even before having constitutionally instituted a government.

Madison argued that such "Bills need not and should not be a part of a constitution." Political preferences prevailed. So, he accommodatingly articulated their inclusion by casting them as a prohibition of interferences in preexisting rights.[2]

Thus,

THE ONE AND ONLY GRANTING OF A RIGHT TO OWN THE LABOR OF YOUR ORIGINALITY, PRACTICE IT AS A USEFUL BUSINESS ART, AND CAUSE PROGRESS IS OF SINGULAR IMPORTANCE!

---

2. More than incidentally, by his inclusion of the particular breadth of subjects of what became those first ten amendments and his influence at excluding others, he persuaded the remaining holdouts of ratification leading to the confirmation of a strengthened Constitution.

This right espouses more than a patent and copyright system. It bespeaks in part the founders' intention to build the American society on its self-supporting economy and to build that economy importantly on the capital of the mind. That freedom and affordability were coexisting intents of our Constitution is overtly declared and inescapably implied.

So, the outreaching propellants of our society that must have seemed like heresies—certainly at least fantasies—to many traditionalists are as follows:

BASIC RIGHTS ARE A GIVEN.

PERSONAL ADVANTAGE IS A CONSTRUCTIVE FORCE.

A LARGE REPUBLIC AND ITS FREEDOMS ARE SUSTAINABLY AFFORDABLE BY PROGRESS IN THE USEFUL ARTS (BUSINESS) BUILT ON SCIENCE.

CONGRESS HAS THE POWER TO PROMOTE THAT PROGRESS.

THE SINGULARITY OF THE ONLY CONSTI-
TUTIONALLY GRANTED RIGHT, THAT DI-
RECTED TO THE ESSENTIAL PROGRESS IN
SCIENCE AND COMMERCE, HAS EXTRA-
ORDINARY MEANING.

With that our story is told. Its enlightenment enlightens us.

This essay reveals and/or refreshes eight
often obscured, history-shaping facts and
a half dozen governance principles that
spawn unassailable benefits to all who
would be free.

Facts

- There was a Scottish Enlightenment.
- Its grandest assembly of scholars advanced the most knowledge per time
  and place.
- Scotland and the colonies were similar as "provinces."

- The Scots targeted religious change here to reform religion at home, which fostered substantial general education in the colonies.
- Scottish thinking stimulated justifiable resistance (revolution) articulating well-reasoned, well-phrased claims for independence not unlike Jefferson's.
- Under Greek governance philosophy, rights had to be earned.
- Under Lockean philosophy, rights are a given.
- Only one right is granted in the body of the U.S. Constitution: to the "property of the mind."

Principles

- A new essential role for commerce in national developments was conceived and emphasized.
- The essence of society is defined.

- Business is the only subsystem of society that generates wealth.
- A large republic breeds factions that mute the tyranny of the majority.
- Self-interest is a force for public good.
- Commerce, capital, and science policies as cornerstone constitutional principles underpin the affordability of a society.

Knowledge of and appreciation of these interrelated facts and basic principles should strengthen our personal enthusiasm and support for our country. The promulgation of these principles to skeptics at home and influential thinkers in other nations can propagate freedom, spawning ground rules for the betterment of the world's continually forming societies.

How Did the Scottish Enlightenment Come to Be?

From whence did spring the Scottish Enlightenment? Was it born of "a sudden burst of genius," as suggested by Dugald Stewart? Stewart was one of the two leading figures, along with Thomas Reid, of the Scottish school of commonsense philosophy and, like some others, a master rhetorician. He knew his question would beg thoughtful answers with extended time dimensions. The knowledge at the time of the history of nature repeatedly confirmed the power of intermittent and evolutionary progress that in this case nurtured the societal environment Stewart and his fellow literati inherited in the 1700s.

Where in time might our story begin? I choose the eve of the Reformation, circa 1500. In the fifteenth century, Scotland was a geographic "identity" that often claimed unto itself its own separateness and independence. Its societal conditions were not unlike the myriad of unjust feudal states and principalities on the continent of Europe and its neighbor and nemesis to the south, England, with whom it fought many wars in the fourteenth and fifteenth centuries. Its religions had been traditional but were becoming contentious. Literacy, overall, was minimal but as prevalent in the more populated areas of Scotland as in most other prominent centers.

The Reformation raised profound questions regarding religion's principles and bias, led by the vigorously articulated (by John Knox among others) Calvinist thesis of God's predetermination of man's predestination in contrast to the humanism thesis of others that God set conditions wherein man can pursue elective intents. The impact of these questions was deeply personal and institutionally destabilizing. Those questions became a dominant preoccupation for the next centuries—but not to the exclusion of other bitter problems. Most sensitive Scot citizens had to bear a lifelong imposition of the self-centered rule of the feudal lords where existent, and the even more self-centered role of the aristocracy of the region and the country. So many local leaders and princes and central monarchs were unprincipled in their governance, as well as scandalous and/or indolent in their public/personal conduct. That was reprehensible. In part, there were cadres of citizens who were numb to a possible reform, while others, led by the literate, began more evidently during the sixteenth century to speak out and write in search of means to resist this sufferance and even hope for change with a moral basis.

In that early era and the century to come, many of the opinion makers were drawn back to ancient scholars such as Plato, Aristotle, and Cicero, while at other times certain thinkers pivoted off the teachings of Erasmus, Machiavelli, Petrarch, and others. Were there keys to answers to then-current problems in the prior lessons? Certain literati credentialed in the Greek and Roman resources hoped for such keys and dared to wonder whether embracing the lessons of classical teaching could earn for Scotland the distinction "The Athens of the North." They seemed to vaguely envision, presciently, the coming of another enlightened age. These labels and hopes, of course, were an overreach, but they measure the dynamics of a meritorious, renewing human intent that steadily strengthened.

It was during this early midmillennium stir that distinct talents ascended to prominence and influence. Of the sixteenth-century scholars, Hector Boece,

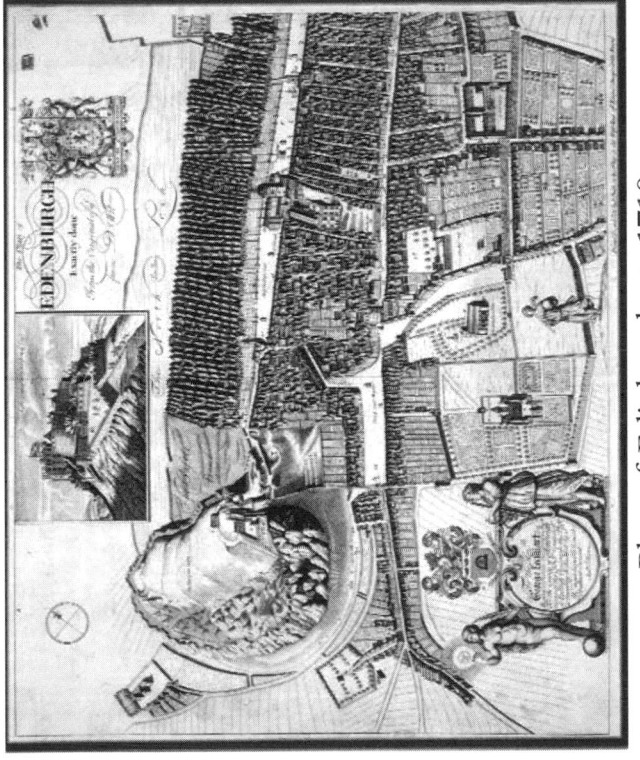

Plan of Edinburgh, c. 1710

View of the High Street of Edinburgh from the East, 1793

The Colledge of Glasgow, c. 1693

John Mair (Major), and George Buchanan were preeminent. Boece was like an intellectual quarterback passing to others the stimulation and inspiration of his fundamental and conservative views on morals and manners. John Major (Mair) attracted a circle of disciples whose effect was widely felt in Scotland, including the emerging institutions of higher learning. His thinking seemed to anticipate the later Enlightenment commonsense school of thought and radiated often to the continent, inviting reciprocal favorable and competing thoughts. Mair's essays had a lasting value, becoming widely studied and in major part adopted by Establishment scholars in the mid-1700s, particularly Thomas Reid.

Buchanan was broadly and sustainingly influential. His capable scholarship was cited repeatedly, including his renowned *History of Scotland,* throughout the next centuries. Illustrative of this was his incisiveness on a fundamental highly supportive of successor Scots' thinking and in tune with the Lockean principles that later influenced our founders. Here is a description of that profundity.

BORROWING FROM CICERO THE THOUGHT THAT THERE WAS A TIME LONG AGO WHEN EARLY MAN ROAMED GOVERNLESS, IT SEEMED CERTAIN TO BUCHANAN THAT "POLITICAL SOCIETY ITSELF HAD EMERGED WHEN MEN DID ASSEMBLE AS THEIR FOND HUMOURS DID LEAD THEM OR SOME COMODITY AND COMON UTILITY DID ALLURE THEM. IF POLITICAL ORGANIZATION WAS THE PRODUCT OF PREVIOUS HUMAN DECISIONS, THEN IT COULD NOT RIGHTLY BE SAID TO BE OF DIVINE ORDINATION. AND IF THIS IS SO, THEN GOVERNMENT OWED ITS VERY LEGITIMACY TO THE FALLIBLE PREFERENCES OF INDIVIDUAL MEN." BUCHANAN NOW FOUND HIMSELF WITH ONLY ONE CONCLUSION AVAILABLE, "THE PEOPLE HAVE THE POWER TO CONFERRE THE GOVERNMENT ON WHOM THEY PLEASE."[1]

---

1. David Allan, *Virtue, Learning and the Scottish Enlightenment* (Edinburgh: Edinburgh University Press, 1993), p. 33.

Many agreed. The sovereignty issue was punctuated early on. Notice Buchanan's elegant, picturesque language. Notice the simple truth he reveals. The dynamics of Scot thinkers' intent was laced with emergent wisdom then and ongoing. Is it any wonder that a grand Enlightenment might evolve should more such thinking prevail?

And more such thinking did prevail! A plodding parade of citizens did steadily swell the ranks of the outspoken. With each generation, new intellectuals would emerge from the ranks, spicing the messages of the masses. Was there now a strengthening set of force fields with a latent magnetism of thinkers begetting thinkers in the seventeenth century and beyond? It proved to be.

On balance, Scotland was evolving a unique combination of cultures and customs, including the following:

1. An emphasis was set on general education. This view was supported by a high interest (for its time) in educa-

tion unto itself. The English, incidentally, favored a specialization education. It was now possible and the time for ordinary men to become better educated and join a chorus for virtue rather than just the privileged obtaining an education.

2. A dual disposition by many was characterized by (a) a strong will to speak out that was paradoxically matched by (b) a healthy quotient of tolerance for others to be heard (not necessarily with agreement, but tolerated).

   Throughout these formative centuries, general tolerance in Scotland was allegedly greater than in some foreign arenas and was frequently cited as being so in the eighteenth century in spite of ongoing vitriolic theological disagreements.

3. The thinking citizens had a natural inclination as to how better to speak out: write history! To the Scots the writing of history was the optimal learning

process. Even the emergent author could observe what was taking place around him, such as the low life of a prince, the injustice of a lord, or an inspiring service in the Kirk. To write the evidence of conditions and possibilities was encouraged and respected.

Appealing means such as these were not lost on each succeeding generation of would-be scholars. Further, expanding on the inspiration of the likes of Boece, Mair, and Buchanan, scores and later hundreds of writers formulated their meaning on the need for high moral principles—virtue—to be applied to unselfish public service and disciplined personal conduct. Most were keenly searching for much improved leadership in and for society. As such, they focused on their prime audience—current and early-prospective civic leaders. In fact, at times when they would interpret that their "leader audience" had grown distant, such as their losing local governance to

London, the advocacy/education energies would wane only to later revitalize. With time, their interests and concerns broadened and deepened with religious differences front and center. It was the myriad of substantial issues responsibly addressed in the sixteenth and particularly the seventeenth centuries that progressively identified Scotland as a welcoming place to be for an intellectual challenge with promising prospects.

The range of subjects crying out for attention and betterment toward the end of the sixteenth century and more so into the seventeenth century included:

RELIGION

HISTORIOGRAPHY

SOCIAL THEORY AND POLITICS

ECONOMICS

ETHICS

LAW

SCIENCE

HUMAN NATURE

AESTHETICS

One other subject that at first mention may strike one as much less significant is language—rhetoric. The early and advancing scholars were mindful of the need to be understood and persuasive. Yet they were often working with an awkward Gaelic vocabulary and language structure whose crudeness had to be refined. Additionally, they had to discern rhetorical devices to gain attention and clarification. At times they would feature an oratorical style of expression. Gradually, many of the interim decades of scholars approached George Buchanan's effective and picturesque speech.

This essay does not dwell on the content and evolving upbeat thinking about each of these topics. However, a few notable factors are sprinkled herein to illustrate the cogency of a new factor complementing or confounding an old one and the increasing recognition of interdisciplinary effects.

We opened our study circa the start of the religious Reformation. Each soul and church was forced to scramble:

- Some in defiance of Catholicism and the pope
- Some puzzled by overproliferation of Protestant claims
- Some retreated to Episcopalian resistance

And on through an almost endless list of what to many of the faithful were heresies breeding acrimony leading even to martyrdom. Above all, Calvinist convictions caused stress on church and state and citizens with unsettling consequences, while winning converts.

Recall that early Calvinism professed the faith that an omnipotent God providentially determined all outcomes. Man was predestined to _____. In contrast, Renaissance humanists accorded man a role to self-intend on his own initiative.

God's role as cast in many of the reforming religions (not exclusively Calvinism) posed profound questions related to the nature of man and his societal associations. These particulars were inseparable from other "divine mysteries" and the ageless political assumption of the divine rights of monarchs. All were subjects for Scottish authors.

Herein was an unparalleled challenge—a complex theological, political, legal, human nature, moral philosophy puzzle worthy of the finest minds who sought for people a better way of life. The setting most compelling to confront the challenge was proving to be Scotland.

Simultaneously, in most of the other subjects crying out for attention, achievements, so often by local countrymen, were also accelerating, attracting serious notice and promising utility. Science and law are instructive illustrations.

The seventeenth century was notable for discoveries in physics, mathematics, and medicine. New knowledge was enthusiastically embraced by a broad range of intellectuals with intent to apply the knowledge, including:

- The philosophy and mathematics of RENÉ DESCARTES (1596–1650). (There were, of course, non-Scottish scholars from whom to learn.)
- The physics and mathematics of ISAAC NEWTON (1642–1727).
- The effect of the founder of a "family dynasty in science," JAMES GREGORY (1638–1675), a friend of Newton's, inventor of the reflecting telescope, first professor of mathematics at the University of Edinburgh. His sons and grandsons followed in his footsteps, filling leading positions as professor of medicine at King College, the medical chair at Edinburgh, and many others.
- DAVID GREGORY (1661–1708), a distinguished astronomer who from 1683

to 1691 was professor of mathematics at the University of Edinburgh, where he taught the theories of Newton prior to their being offered in England. The entire Gregory circle was awesome.

- SIR ROBERT SIBBALD (1641–1722), who played an integral role in Edinburgh's prominence in medicine. Sibbald studied on the continent, as did other scholars, and brought his skills back to Scottish centers. He was joined by notable contemporary colleagues such as James Halket and Archibald Petcairne.

These individuals as well as significant others ensured that the rest of the world of science and scholars in general could not ignore Scot thinking.

The sophistication of the law was evolving in many countries, and Scotland was motivated to keep up. Sir James Dalrymple (later Viscount Stair, 1616–1695) and

Sir George Mackenzie (1636–1691) were senior leaders and teachers. Stair was expert in civil law; Mackenzie was renowned in criminal law. They were able teachers and practitioners who honorably borrowed unashamedly from top legal minds on the continent, such as Samuel Pufendorf, whose teaching also influenced Francis Hutcheson (who virtually launched the Scottish Enlightenment). But even their best efforts left an opening for their successors to blend and upgrade advanced theses of social theory, politics, ethics, and rhetoric into a strong case for Scotland to stand eventually as a peer to other nations "before the Bar."

Of course, the quintessential law in any country is its constitution. It is axiomatic in most countries that to the judiciary is vested the power of declaring and enforcing the superior power of a constitution as the supreme law of a land. A preeminent twentieth-century member of the Scottish judiciary, Lord Cameron, recently opined that the early Scottish concept of the hierarchical standing of the judiciary over the legislature in determining the constitutionality of a law may have influenced the approved provision in the U.S. Constitution. He noted that at least up to the Union of 1707, the determinative interpretation within Scotland's legal system rested with the Supreme Courts of Scotland. Stair had relevantly observed earlier, "We differ from the English whose statutes of Parliament of whatsoever antiquity remain ever in force until they be repealed." Herein we Americans learn of another likely influence by prior generations of Scots on a key principle among the separation of powers.

In varying but mostly lofty degrees, advances in Scottish thinking on all the major subjects were both increasingly creditable and continuously welcoming the augmentation from the circles around Montesquieu, Voltaire, Rousseau, Kant, and others. But as the eighteenth century loomed, no other circle addressed "the whole" as did the scholars in Scotland, whose full circle of thinking was reinforcing a set of national qualities unparalleled elsewhere. These national qualities were as follows:

- The most hospitable and stimulating environment for scholarship
- A well-developed aggregation of open-minded universities
- The maturing of knowledge in most topics that promised accelerated learning and its application
- A history of virtually breeding more and better scholars who relayed their talents to successors over almost three centuries
- A captivating momentum that seemed to refuel itself

Within this hearty general and academic environment, learned men, generations in the making, stepped forth in the eighteenth century, spoke up one scholar after another, and became in the aggregate the Enlightenment.

Dugald Stewart knew it didn't spring as a sudden burst. It rooted and gestated over time. It was not the product of a single genius. It was the product of the maturing genius of a people.

Leaderless, for the most part, they had put themselves in motion individually. Without realizing it, they became more self-organized. Today we have a better understanding of an ageless fundamental phenomenon of nature: most complex activities and entities naturally, almost subliminally, organize themselves. In this case, the people's irrepressible tenacity and high value intent energized the inconspicuous, continuous, self-organizing process.

And so it was that the stage was set and the casting for the Scottish Enlightenment (1720–1780) came to be.

—∞∞—

The rest of life in the first decades of the 1700s was ongoing with nary a hint that an enlightenment was unfolding. What was apparent was that major distractions were rampant. Some were the nagging broodings over earlier injury to national pride:

- The Scots had lost their own royal court when the Crowns of Scotland and England were united barely a hundred years earlier, in 1603.
- Then in 1707 they lost their parliament to London.
- Only a few years earlier, the established powers in Scotland had planned (the Darien Scheme) to establish a colony in Central America that failed miserably and drained critical resources.
- The country was yet to be rocked by the futile rebellions against London in 1715 and 1745.

But the greater distractions to the ordinary citizenry were dire living conditions and unsavory working conditions, including in the emerging commercial sector. A strenuous reaction to deplorable human conditions could easily blunt support for future grand intents. We would learn that these deep concerns would not go unheeded by the learned "thinkers who would be doers," such as Adam Smith, David Hume, and the many ethicists.

A short digression here will place in context as a final insight a set of relevant issues illustrating how the enlightened aimed to influence contemporary and future transcending outcomes.

Worldly thinkers, influenced importantly by Adam Ferguson, understood that the societal development of man had developed through four stages, simply summarized as hunter-gatherers, herders, farmers, and men of commerce. What the Enlightenment thinkers were adding to the basics was the broadened understanding of the complex role of property:

- Hunter-gatherers consumed their edibles daily.
- Herders' possessions were almost constantly on the move.
- Farmers settled on land, used tools, and held inventory.
- Commercial ownerships were more complicated.

Principles, policies, and laws concerning property—and now working conditions—demanded clear thinking and resolutions.

The enlightened addressed these stage-by-stage factors and the day-to-day conditions not as a distraction that might inhibit hopes for betterment but as an opportunity to orchestrate betterment. That they succeeded in large measure by showing the way to seeding the means to afford the application of their new tangible and conceptional enlightened knowledge is attested to by the endorsement of Jay G. Prokop, repeated here from "The Untold Story" essay:

THE GREAT ACHIEVEMENT OF THE SCOTTISH SCHOOL OF SOCIOLOGICAL HISTORIANS WAS THE RECOGNITION THAT A COMMERCIAL ORGANIZATION OF SOCIETY HAD RENDERED OBSOLETE MUCH THAT HAD BEEN BELIEVED ABOUT SOCIETY BEFORE.

Dr. David Allan, author of *Virtue, Learning and the Scottish Enlightenment,* takes the Prokop testimonial meaning on to a virtual summary of this essay's story. He writes:

THE HISTORY OF PROPERTY WHICH CHARACTERIZED THE HISTORICAL SCHOLARSHIP OF EIGHTEENTH CENTURY SCOTLAND MAY THUS BE UNDERSTOOD ONLY AS A SPECIAL CASE IN A LONGER CUL-

TURAL CONTINUUM. IT WAS ENHANCED BY CONTEMPORARY ECONOMIC AND INTELLECTUAL TRENDS, BUT WAS CONSISTENT STILL WITH THE SLOWLY EVOLVING SCOTTISH EXPLORATION OF MORALITY AND MANNERS BEGUN BY HECTOR BOECE.[2]

2. Allan, *Virtue, Learning and the Scottish Enlightenment,* p. 164.

Postscript:
Unintended Consequences

Early in the essay "How Did the Scottish Enlightenment Come to Be?" I credit the initiators of Scottish intellectual renewal with meritorious intent. Although their wish to gain eventual recognition for their country as an Athens of the North was an overreach, it did bespeak a grand intent seeded with quality thinking and exposition even then. That was circa the 1500s.

Before 1800, the common demeanor of so many of the intellectual elite—even the credentialed enlightened authorities who had prolifically produced profound, inter-related, intellectual jewels in their her-alded time—questioned man's ability to conceive and fulfill grand intents. It was not as if they individually derated their self-confidence. On the contrary, many manifested exaggerated self-esteem, which may have helped support their of-ten evident low evaluation (undeserved) of the scholarship of their predecessors. They did sustain their individual and inter-dependent scholarship.

The Calvinist thesis of divine predeter-mination now infected most thinking. According to that thesis, the basic path-way of life was laid out, and mankind's potential to change it and its byways sig-nificantly would at most be "uninten-tional." If notable achievements would ever be forthcoming, they would be di-vinely enabled as "special Providences." In the context of the then "theory of un-intended consequences," the idiom unin-tended consequence seemed to mean major consequences cannot flow from man's conscious rational intent. In the normal course of performing his predestined course of activities, man can make a difference, but the consequence is likely to be marginal and unintended. Even to a devout Calvinist, such a characterization could have had a demoralizing effect. To this day, scholars of the Enlightenment are seeking to better understand the effect of this infection on the potential output of the Enlightened during their prime—the mid-eighteenth century—and its possible effect on the waning influence of and eventual demise of the Enlightenment in the nineteenth century.

It would seem reasonable that the festering infection could have de-energized scholastic momentum and its application at least partially in the latter part of the eighteenth century and even more likely tempered advancement at the turn of the century. Fortunately, substantial inspirational and instructional lessons did flow to our prospective founders at beneficial times.

— ∞ —

Even if the Calvin effect had not occurred, new, powerful, and disquieting political, military, economic, and philosophical phenomena were stirring in England and the continent by the early nineteenth century. A continuing Scots-driven intellectual renaissance was probably unlikely.

— ∞ —

Unintended consequences can deliver transcending benefits and, yes, problems, too. Elective intents (consequences) with transcending purpose can be conceived and are fulfillable. In our time this is the faith from our fathers and within ourselves.

The case has been made in these essays that our forefathers—our founders—were blessed with a cascade of wisdom and practical guidance from the Scots that was more than just seasoning to their recipe for good government. Of course, our founders' educations were from a variety of sources, but would it ever have been complete and timely without, for example:

BUCHANAN   The people have the power
                  to conferre the government
                  on whom they please

HUTCHESON   The right to resistance
ET AL.   The role of virtue

HUME   A large republic will sustain
                  freedom

TEACHERS   Madison, Jefferson, Hamilton
FROM   so tutored by age sixteen
SCOTLAND   William Small's prime
                  influence on Jefferson
             John Witherspoon, mentor to
                  Madison

REID, PAINE, RUSH	The common sense of "common sense"
SMITH, WATT, HUTTON, BLACK, CULLEN, MILLER, ET AL.	Economic and science vitalization available for United States to take advantage
SCOTTISH SCHOOL OF SOCIO- LOGICAL HISTORIANS	The new role for commerce and property in civilly founding and affording a nation
THE LAW	Scot courts' constitutional authority vs. statutes of parliament of whatsoever antiquity remaining

None of these Enlightenment masters and their many colleagues intended a founding of the United States of America. Yet, individually and collectively their unintended consequence made a giant difference in that most important founding.

Thus, we relearn. Do not underestimate the leverage of the product of scholar-selected-scholarship nor demean the power of man to build to a much better life for mankind. Even unintended consequences leave transcending legacies.

Illustration Acknowledgments

SCOTTISH PENNY COMMEMORATING
ADAM SMITH (pp. iii–iv)

Courtesy The Art Archive/British Museum

JAMES WATT (p. 12)

by Partridge

*Courtesy Library of Congress, Prints and
Photographs Division*

ADAM SMITH (p. 13)

by John Kay

*Courtesy Library of Congress, Prints and
Photographs Division*

FRANCIS HUTCHESON (p. 14)

by F. Bartolozzi

Courtesy the Newberry Library, Chicago

DAVID HUME (p. 15)

Courtesy Hulton/Archive Photos

THOMAS JEFFERSON (p. 23)

by Cornelius Tiebout

Courtesy Library of Congress, Prints and Photographs Division

JAMES MADISON (p. 24)

by David Edwin

Courtesy Library of Congress, Prints and Photographs Division

ALEXANDER HAMILTON (p. 25)

by Thomas Hamilton Crawford

Courtesy Library of Congress, Prints and Photographs Division

JOHN WITHERSPOON (p. 26)

by Charles Wilson Peale

Courtesy Library of Congress, Prints and Photographs Division

WILLIAM SMALL (p. 27)

Courtesy The Assay Office, Birmingham, England

PLAN OF EDINBURGH, C. 1710 (p. 53)

by Andrew Johnston

Courtesy the Stapleton Collection

VIEW OF THE HIGH STREET OF
EDINBURGH FROM THE EAST, 1793 (p. 54)

by David Allan

*Courtesy City of Edinburgh Museums and Art
Galleries, Scotland/Bridgeman Art Library*

THE COLLEDGE OF GLASGOW, C. 1693 (p. 55)

by John Slezer

Courtesy the Newberry Library, Chicago

Index

About the Author

I never knew personal financial hardship. But those around me did. When my mother and father were rendered penniless and jobless in my first year, Uncle Jack, a Chicago policeman, and Aunt Helen took us into their tiny one-room, inner-door-bed apartment for three weeks. When I was a teenager, whenever we would enthusiastically visit them, I was awed that the five of us had survived such crowding. Is it any wonder that my folks avowed "Never forget your old relatives"? My sensitive wife, Mary, instinctively took the lead to reach out tirelessly to both our relatives.

By the time I was eight, we had our own modest two-bedroom apartment in Chicago. Each year for a series of years, circa 1930, we would move a few blocks to an almost identical layout. By then I took part in family chores and could pack the dishes in the barrel for the movers and take down and put up curtains. All hands, mom, dad, and son, were involved. Why the regular moves? I wondered. The cost of the move was ten dollars. As I learned later, each new lease was negotiated with two months' free rent! This net savings was vital to my folks. Life went on for me, but with more meaning.

I was destined to be a boss's son. My father had started fledgling Motorola in 1928. He took me on exciting introductory business trips as a little boy—a paddle-wheel boat to the next distributor, an early airplane ride, and more. He had me give the banquet speech at his tenth anniversary car radio convention in 1940 when I was a senior in high school as a symbol that there would be a future after the war for his customers and employees. Even then, I was an accomplished public speaker. Time after time he would provide me such challenges that manifested trust. Trust has been the consummate value in our family to this day.

My enlistment in the Signal Corps was beneficial. My return into the ranks of the company provided the base from which I could earn my business credentials This led to an ever-so-satisfying fifty years of service to and with my associates—thirty of those years as chief of the company.

Public service opportunities were offered, which I selectively performed, with the support of a loving and accomplished wife, the mother of our four responsible children.

All of these and other privileges and duties were optimally consummated within the heartening environment endowed by the principals of the Founding and vitalized by family principles.

America's
Founding Secret

Interior design by
LORI ROBLIN

Composed by
ROWMAN & LITTLEFIELD PUBLISHING GROUP
in Adobe Garmond Light
with display lines in
Opti Dianna Script Light

Printed in the United States of America by
EDWARDS BROTHERS, INCORPORATED
on 70-pound EB Natural paper

Smythe-sewn by
EDWARDS BROTHERS, INCORPORATED
in a three-piece case using
Rainbow Black spine and Rainbow Café side panels